NOW I CAN TELL

NOW I CAN TELL

Poems from St John's Hospice

Edited by
Lynne Alexander

with a foreword by Douglas Dunn

and photographs by
Ian Beesley

MACMILLAN

First published in 1990 by
PAPERMAC
a division of Macmillan Publishers Limited
4 Little Essex Street London WC2R 3LF
and Basingstoke

Associated companies in Auckland, Delhi, Dublin, Gaborone, Hamburg, Harare,
Hong Kong, Johannesburg, Kuala Lumpur, Lagos, Manzini, Melbourne, Mexico City,
Nairobi, New York, Singapore and Tokyo

ISBN 0–333–53129–9

A CIP catalogue record for this book is available from the British Library

Photoset by Rowland Phototypesetting Limited
Bury St Edmunds, Suffolk
Printed by
WBC Limited, Bristol and Maesteg

This publication is supported by North West Arts

This book is dedicated to all its contributors

We are dying, we are dying, so all we can do
is now to be willing to die, and to build the ship
of death to carry the soul on the longest journey.

A little ship, with oars and food
and little dishes, and all accoutrements
fitting and ready for the departing soul.

D. H. Lawrence
from 'The Ship of Death'

Acknowledgements

I would like to thank: Sister Ainé Cox, Dr Malcolm McIllmurray and the staff of St John's Hospice; Dr Terry McCormick for suggesting the idea of a Writer in Residence; Dr David Gorst for making the project happen and for being its mainstay; Dr Ann Morris, Project Co-ordinator, for getting the project off the ground, and for her sensitivity and friendship; Jean Argles, for her help; Meg McCaldin, for her energy and clarity and belief in the project; David Downes and Liz Yorke for their support; North West Arts, Lancashire County Council, Lancaster City Council, The Frieda Scott Charitable Trust, The Francis C. Scott Charitable Trust, The King's Fund, and South Lakeland District Council for their financial support.

Foreword

One of the reasons why poetry exists is that it says something about the emotional lives we have in common. Love, grief, joy, sorrow, fear, delight in nature, pleasure, indignation, loathing, remorse, pain, dejection, vitality, courage and faint-heartedness are among these feelings and states of mind and body which encompass the range of human experience. They can be expressed in whatever manner truth demands, according to circumstances. Although you might not think so were you to read contemporary criticism, poetry is a remarkably open art. Its governing attitudes and styles and forms vary according to the temperaments of those who write it. Poetry presents a capacity for its own democratic inclusiveness. Anyone can try this art. Its artistic requirements are enormous, but they should never be considered as barriers.

Whether to read or write, or both, many people turn to poetry in moments of personal crisis. Love and grief are perhaps the most common of the upheavals that force men and women to express themselves on paper. It is not just that poetry is the handiest literary form that leads people to it. There is something about poetry itself that is understood by people unaccustomed to reading and writing verse. Attempts to explain this phenomenon would have us believe that it has something to do with memories of poems read at school. Personally, I feel that this amounts to a reflex operated by the guardians of Literature (with a capital L). When men and women for whom poetry has played no great part in their lives are moved to write by love, sorrow or the prospect of death, then the compulsion has to be explained in terms more fundamental to life than those offered by the routine vocabulary of literature. It is intuitive; and it might even be inexplicable. Nor is the social function of art demeaned should we describe the urge to participate in it as mysterious. It is an intimate but not necessarily private ceremonial. Most of the writing in this collection, for example, is quite clearly directed at others. People turn to poetry at heightened moments of life because poetry imitates the drama of what is being lived.

Serious illness, the approach of death, or the awareness of a loved one's dying are among these heightened moments when every hour counts and each morning is unexpected. When men and women are confronted with these experiences, and, unfamiliar with poetry, they write it, then what they indicate is that poetry is a far more natural activity than our society cares to make out. Or perhaps it is not just poetry that is seen to be on the fringes of allegedly greater priorities, but candour, anything that touches the truths of life and death on the quick.

Death, dying and the grief of survivors are embedded in taboos; and taboos are themselves the expressions of a covert consensus to which, in all likelihood, we subscribed before the experience of nursing a loved one, and then the experience of grief. What we witness in nursing, followed by the reactions of friends and strangers to grief, are what expose these taboos for what they are – a form of embarrassment which holds at arm's length both the fear of death and the dread of bereavement; it is a syndrome which insists that the unthinkable remains unthought.

These poems penetrate taboos and discard embarrassment. Their testimonies, which are always at grips with their authors' resistant identities, make no great claims to art. They do not need to. Honesty and truthfulness are more than enough. They offer their own insights into the minds of the dying and the love of those who will survive them.

I know, or knew, none of these writers; but the memory they have given me of them is an experience I consider precious.

Douglas Dunn

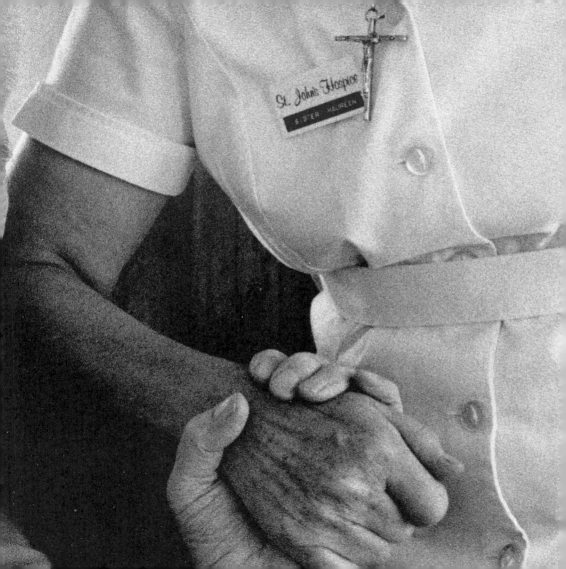

The Hospice

I suppose all hospices are extraordinary places but we in Lancaster feel that St John's is very special indeed. The astonishing generosity of local people provided the money to build it and it seemed almost as if Sister Ainé and her colleagues were waiting in the wings to work there.

It is run as a charitable trust with some of the costs borne by the Health Authority but a continuous input from local people and organisations. The Medical Director is Dr M. B. McIllmurray and the Matron, Sister Ainé Cox, whose order (The Sisters of our Lady of the Apostles) provides many of the nurses. Many posts in the Hospice are filled by volunteers.

It is a calm, spacious building, filled with light and surrounded by green things. Apart from being a place where people who are dying may be looked after, the Hospice exists for chronically ill patients who may be admitted for periods of a few weeks. Many patients have only a short time left to them when they are admitted but some will become well enough to go home and perhaps come in several times. Others may visit the Hospice whilst in remission from their disease or after being cured. Many of the meetings and events of the CancerCare support organisation take place at St John's. The contributors include not only hospice patients: one is a receptionist, some are nurses, some relatives, and others are people who came for CancerCare activities.

Right from the beginning, St John's has been full of life and people getting on with the business of living. It has rapidly become a prominent feature of the community and we often wonder how on earth we managed before it was there.

The Doctor

Why does a doctor involve himself in a literature project? It is not easy to explain but platitudes about communication and art really only serve to cover up the real reason, which is that I am hooked on the written word. What relief it is to enter another world simply by opening a book. If you are faced repeatedly with distress and disease, then you do need to be able to escape. You can climb mountains (I do), you can take a drink (I do), you can offload your problems on to others (I don't), but best of all you can just switch off, shuck all responsibility and become a reader. Now, like most addicts, I will go to extraordinary lengths to get access to the drug and to involve others in the habit; I am fascinated by the details and process of production of the intoxicant. You can see that this whole project was for me so close to the process of creative writing and it has been quite wonderful.

Doctors see things that others do not. By this I do not mean only that we are permitted to examine people and their constituent parts in curious ways and unusual circumstances. Whilst this is true, I also think that we are trained observers who look and really see. This doctor has been involved in the treatment of malignant disease for more than fifteen years and he has looked and seen and remembered. He is sometimes troubled by ghosts. He is under no illusions about the limitations of many of the treatments and has thought for some time that terminal care must be more than bedpans, morphine and mouth-washes – important as these things are. To help patients experience

new things, reach new understanding of themselves and even create something of lasting value in the final phase of their life – these were the aims of this project. Even if we failed, we succeeded in that each patient was treated as a very special person and this is the way it should be.

Part of the purpose of this book is that we may remember the people whose work is included. Some are dead now but their families will, I hope, be pleased and proud to see what has been created. Those patients who read the book and see their own writings may feel a little shy at being exposed so, but take it from me, there is nothing to worry about: the reader should feel privileged to be allowed this glimpse of the real you.

Finally a word about Lynne. She is many things: an author, a teacher, a former counsellor. When we appointed her to the residency we did not realise how well we had chosen. She is small and American but nice. We became friends. I worried about her being exposed to illness and death at every turn. You can lose your perspective and your way so easily, living in and breathing the supercharged emotional atmosphere of the Hospice. You think everyone is going to die – well, they are of course:

> Dear doctor, shall I die?
> Yes my dear, and so shall I.

But I need not have worried. She is resilient and she has the priceless gift of a self-deprecating sense of humour. She is fun. Somehow, we all have the feeling that she has always been here and, because she is comfortable to be with, open, trusting and honest, the contributors to this book have blossomed. If this project has been a success, if this book has any merit, then it is because Lynne put her heart into it.

I cannot understand how the magic was worked (although it was all done before our eyes, no deception, nothing up the sleeve), but suddenly poetry was everywhere. It seemed everyone was writing poetry and poetry was not an airy-fairy art form found in slim volumes with limp covers, but was pouring out of young and old, educated and illiterate, patients, nurses – everyone. I had not expected it to be poetry for some reason, but I am glad it was.

Read the poems, look at the wonderful pictures of the patients and remember or get to know the people; see the world through their eyes, understand what they felt and share their pains and their pleasures.

David Gorst

The Father

[Terry McCormick is Resident Curator for the Wordsworth Trust in Grasmere and the person who first suggested having a writer in residence at St John's. In the following, he writes about his son's illness and eventual death from leukaemia, and his own involvement with the St John's Literature Project.]

Perhaps Rowan's greatest pleasure was listening to stories; especially those which were 'out of your mouth'. Those that were made up. The all-time favourite was *Peter the Pike* which began its life before Rowan was diagnosed with leukaemia in the summer of 1984.

Peter the Pike was an angry and apparently ferocious creature who terrorised all forms of life in the upper reaches of the Rivers Duddon and Esk. But when he arrived at the pure blue pool where Rowan and his tribe – water babes all of them – played and held sway, he met his match and was, after many battles, successfully resisted.

Much of the power of this story, as in any, was in the telling. But now, as I reflect, I can see this tale called up an aura of innocence and paradise for all of us before Rowan's childhood was slammed away when he was three and a half years old.

Peter the Pike became a sort of talisman. When Rowan was in crisis he would whisper his demand: 'Tell me the story of *Peter the Pike*.' And we would go through it. As though coping with this crazy, glaring, angry, trouble-seeking creature was a metaphor for coping with leukaemia.

By the time Rowan had relapsed in the autumn of 1986, Peter, banished from the Duddon, had further adventures in his quest for trouble up and down the River Esk; especially with two brothers – Rowan and Tangwyn – who lived in a house with a garden running down to the river near Boot. These adventures led Peter the Pike to the open sea where he swam out towards the horizon without direction, still glaring angrily back at the two boys who watched him from the shore.

And there were so many other stories; a richness of myth and poetry through which all of us – Julia, Tangwyn, Rowan, myself – could breathe a little.

In September 1987 it became possible to manage aspects of Rowan's treatment under Drs Gorst and Matthews and the team at Lancaster. Closer to home, our thoughtfulness about our dilemma seemed more significant if only because it could be more usefully applied. So the suggestion (no, more a question), 'Why don't you have a writer in residence at St John's Hospice?' now seems obvious, given our experience as a family and my work as Curator for the Wordsworth Trust. It was David Gorst's immediate enthusiasm for this suggestion which influenced my own involvement, alongside Ann Morris, in the development of the project throughout 1988.

Rowan's other great passion besides stories and the telling of stories was bird life; birds of prey; and especially eagles. His knowledge of these creatures was, as all those who knew him will testify, immense and precocious. The number and colour of tail feathers, the length of talon, the exact curve of beak; here was an intellectual mastery which was matched by his capacity to identify with birds of prey and particularly the eagle, the Golden Eagle of Scotland and the Lake District.

In the early summer of 1988, following a conversation of cathartic honesty with his mother, Julia, Rowan knew he was going to die. He was straightforward. He wanted his body to be left on a ledge on Nab Scar above the secret place from which he had seen a young eagle and, frequently, the stoop of peregrines. Birds of prey and the eagle could then consume his remains.

During the last weeks, stories and their telling became more and yet more important. And there was Peter the Pike still swimming out to sea. One evening, having gone through the story again, Rowan asked me to finish it; what was going to happen to Peter? I could not do this and said I couldn't. Rowan sat up and told his own ending . . .

As Peter swam out to sea, some Sea Eagles which nested on the cliffs saw his angry eye glaring and flew out wheeling and diving. The Pike did not see them before their talons sank into the back of his head. The Sea Eagles carried the Pike off to their ledge and then ate him and fed him to their offspring.

Rowan died two weeks later on 3 September 1988; he was seven years and ten months old.

Terry McCormick

The Writer-in-Residence

Elizabeth is the last person with whom I shall work. She is in her early forties. She has had multiple sclerosis for twenty-two years but it has become much worse recently. She is a musician but can no longer play; she cannot walk. Writing tires her but she can use a word-processor. She tells me that after she left St John's this time she went home to spend the weekend with her man, but that on the last morning she woke to find him dead.

What does one say? How can I help?

'I want to write about it but I don't know how.'

'I'll come and see you and we can talk about it.'

Alec was the first. He was full of words. He'd been in one of the Queen's regiments at Windsor Castle during the war. (He had so much to say: should I use a tape recorder or just make notes or what?) We made a date to get together as soon as I got back from holiday. I told him I was looking forward to it and meant it. He was dead when I got back.

Quite early on in the project, Granada Television made a film about the project. One of the questions they asked me – a rather peculiar one – was, Did I like working with death: wasn't it depressing? Nobody likes working with death, I said, but then I wasn't working with death; I was working with people, some of whom happened to be at the end of their lives. While it could on occasion be disturbing, saddening, awe-inspiring and sometimes terrible to sit beside those who were jaundiced or palsied or tumorous or just too thin for words, it was never ever depressing. Why not? Because no matter how ill they were, when people were talking, feeling, remembering, choosing words – an unconventional kind of writing but writing nevertheless – they were too busy being alive to be either depressed or depressing.

Poetry dripping from the lips like honey? Hardly. Words, memories and random thoughts more often came out in dribbles; in mumbled, halting, whispered snatches often accompanied by tears and apologies. I held a lot of hands and cried along. But there were plenty of giggles and smiles too.

What did I actually do? Mostly I sat and listened and with permission took notes. When it seemed relevant I talked about my own quadruple bereavement. A connection was established. When something somebody said caught my attention I'd say, 'Listen to that, you could write a poem about that . . . or put this together with that . . .' and so on. 'Oh, I couldn't write poetry,' would come the inevitable reply. 'You can,' I'd say, 'I'll show you.'

Sometimes I suggested opening lines such as 'I remember', 'I wish' and so on; but when I got more confident I let people set their own beginnings. When it came to the actual writing, I took many liberties. I edited, pared down, isolated or framed certain images; I tried to give shape to random utterances. I was amanuensis, teacher, word plumber if you like. A colleague called it putting my libretto to their opera. A collaboration, a co-journey; what you will.

The other day I revisited the Hospice. The poems, I noted, were still up on the corridor wall. I let myself remember how family, friends, relatives stood around pointing and musing. 'Have you seen that one?' . . . 'That's the one that really gets me . . .' The poems put into words what they felt but didn't dare or know how to say. Memories were jogged, emotions stirred. All that was good. By the end of the project the idea of poetry around St John's had changed from some remote, rather terrifying thing that had to do with school and great dead male writers to something any of us could do if we had a mind to. It pleased me to see it go tumbling off its pedestal of high culture and into the everyday world of the Hospice.

It was the patients themselves of course who most liked seeing their work displayed. 'I never thought anyone would want to read anything I had to say,' said Arthur Marshall. He pushed his wheelchair out into the corridor and smiled, then went back to his bed and died. I wheeled Gladys McCartan out to read hers. She scowled, 'That's it, that's how it was.' I overheard John Shaw, the biggest sceptic of all, say to his niece, 'Have you read my poems?' Clara Blyton said, 'I've got to eighty and somebody's interested in me. It's too funny for words.'

Now the project is over it is all too easy to lose heart. The subjects should have been grander, perhaps more spiritual; we should have been privy to more Great Last Thoughts Before Death; more dark nights of the soul. An Abercrombie suit, a song ('Yes, We Have No Bananas'), the line 'For a Communist she made wonderful porridge', the dreaded chemotherapy – what's all this mundanity? Have we failed in the spiritual stakes? I think not. Of course inspired visions are great when you can get them, but these small offerings are sweeter. Let this book be a celebration of them and of the people who gave voice to them.

This book is dedicated to all those people with whom I am so privileged and proud to have worked.

Lynne Alexander

The Patients, Staff and Relatives

Olive Ward

Who is that lady in the pink robe who seems so in charge of herself and who holds court in her cubicle every afternoon to so many visitors? Sister Ward, senior staff nurse at The Royal Lancaster Infirmary's surgical ward. She has only just been told she has cancer and is having a brief stay at the Hospice while waiting for her treatment to begin. Last week an important member of staff, now a patient. I can't help thinking it must be a special kind of torture for a woman like Olive – normally in charge of other people's illnesses – to be in the helpless position she is in. No wonder she sits in the corner in that brittle, flinching way, taking the measure of her visitors.

Visitors

Car Key Types. They arrive breathless
twirling the car key ring in one hand –
'only staying for two minutes'
then sit down and stay for ages.

Afternoon Tea Types. They arrive quite slowly
dressed in British Home Stores dresses
with cardigans over their arms.
They reorganise all the chairs in the room,
sit down, look very comfortable –
one could imagine
any minute a flask and picnic
will come out of the bag.

The Questioners. They attack with questions:
how, when, where? One feels
a tape-recorded message would help.

The Embarrassed. They don't know what to say.
They look very serious and bothered,
they attack with the most boring stories:
mother-in-law, children and holidays.

The Gangs. Six turn up one morning
they don't know each other
I have to introduce them
try to keep the conversation going
play hostess. I don't feel like it –
I feel weary, cornered.
If the big windows had been opened
I would have felt like falling out.

The Selfish. The writer in residence
comes along at ten to two every day
preventing me from watching *Neighbours*.

The Normal. Edith, Dorothy and Mum.
They don't make demands
don't ply questions
always behave quite normally:
they treat you as the person you are.

Colin Stones

Pale, bald, leather-jacketed; holey jeans, motorbike helmet tucked under his arm; hunched in a corner. When he stands he towers over me. I think, uh oh. He mumbles a few incomprehensible words. Then he smiles (whew). Two minutes later I'm smiling too; two hours later I'm hugging him and practically dancing round the place. Colin is pleased too. He says, 'I woke up this morning an ordinary Col [Colin] and I'm going out of here a poet.'

Bone marrow transplant followed by some kind of infection. He looks like death, sleeps away the days. What use is poetry now?

Good Friday, I'm convinced Colin will die. I curse the sun; go up to Eskdale and fall in a bog. Pluck up courage to go and see him on Easter Monday and find him guzzling Pepsi and ice cream and having escape fantasies. I should have known.

Colin is 'cured' (dare I say it?). He's gone to the TT races on the Isle of Man. His hair has grown, he's the colour of a strong cup of PG Tips. His eyes twinkle and he has that funny little smirky smile back. He spends time with his mates, works on his bikes and cars. He's learning silversmithing.

What has writing meant to him? 'I was game for a laugh. My hands were wrecked, I couldn't turn a spanner so I thought, right, might as well push a pen. I met Lynne . . . and we ended up creating something in the region of a poem.'

Oh aye.

Shock

Queuing at the bank
I was feeling watched
gammy and self-conscious
I was tall
There was a lot of middle-aged housewives
standing about in their flat shoes
I felt a nudge in my back
I spun round on my heels – what's up?
This blue-rinsed lady
with her eyebrows on her nose
and her I'm-about-to-ask-you-a-big-deep-question face says:
'Why does a young lad like you shave his head?'
'It's not shaved, it fell out'
She looked at me with a why-face
she didn't say anything
Then I said, 'I've got cancer'
There were no more comments
just a whole row of oh-my-god faces.

Hair

Curly mop
flopped about
made itself noticed.
It's good to have hair
that's tickling your chin
you feel it's there.
Now it's gone I feel naked
when it first got shaved off
it really bothered me.
Now I enjoy it
all those people look at you.

Ward 3 Pink Suite

Kippin' on a plank
aching limbs
boredom
body's sore
corners getting flattened in.

Staring at the ceiling –
somewhere to park your eyes
so's your mind can bugger off.
Pack it up and roll over
go up a wall or a cupboard
for a change of scenery.

All this horrendous food getting me down
rubber chips, dodgy puddings.
Tied to a drip,
sucking on thermometers,
wrapping a bit of junk round your arm –
yes, he's still alive.

This liver infection is getting me down
this body is getting me down.
Time to roll over again.

Red Cells, White Cells and Clotted Cells

All taken for granted –
charge round
day in, day out
nobody ever thinks twice
until one day
you give yourself a slice –
and it's running away from you.

Being My Illness

I could be moping in and out
– give him such and such a drug –
I remember going for a ride
a portion of normality
in an otherwise wrecked life
then back to the illness.

I used to rip to work through traffic.
Now I turn the bike round
and head for the country instead –
a much better experience altogether.
That's when I start feeling
like a human being again.
I don't have to live
within my illness anymore
it makes me feel normal.
One of the biggest things makes it a thrill
is the fact that all the doctors say
you shouldn't be doing that.

But what do they know
about the therapeutic value
of a good blast on a bike?

New Era

If I hadn't been ill
everything would've been bland
day in day out
get on with the job.
I took it for granted.
Now I have this
it's told me:
you want to be doing something –
college, learning,
welding, photography,
get back into taking pictures.
I'd like to write.
I want to improve myself
become independent
make something out of myself.
The next stage will be good
when my hair grows.
I can put my boots on
and ride to where I want
when I want.
Then it'll be the beginning
of a new era.

I gotta do something
before my head cabbages.

So

I'm very so.
People say,
   if you do so-and-so
   something super-bad will happen
   and I say, so what?

The whole order's changed now.

What's not important:
   money
   power
   winning (I don't rate it as super-important; I used to).

What is important:
   to be free (you can be free on your feet, on a train, on your
      pushbike or just in your mind);
   to do what you want when you want;
   to do it in good health (no use trying to do it on one leg).

John Shaw

John sits with his white cane parked beside him and his hands folded over his substantial stomach like the Hospice guru enjoying a private joke. Sometimes he holds court with other day-care patients or one of the sisters, or sits on his own drinking tea and looking thoughtful, or has a snooze with his head on his chest like a pouter pigeon.

John is one of the walking wounded. How does the smile keep from sliding off his face? He's blind, he's got cancer, arthritis, paralysis, maybe even gout – you name it. He's lost two wives, his daughter has disowned him; what more, as he says, can go wrong? He swings his cane à la Fred Astaire, chuckles, pats his tummy and winks: nothing to do but carry on so you might as well enjoy it.

Humour is his trump card and undoubtedly his best medicine. He laughs at his pain, at his old dicky body, at his doctors, at himself, at me, at all of us, at life.

What I Can See

I can see a face, hair at the top
because it's darker
after that I can see nothing at all
I can see the paper you're writing on: it's white
I can see a discrepancy between your feet –
they're darker than the chair
but what colour they are I couldn't tell you:
black, blue, brown – I just can't tell.

I can see that white curtain
I can see the fawn carpet
I can see a black and white roofline
but I can't see the sky
this light is obliterating the sky.

Doctor's Visit

I sit in the chair,
he sits on the settee
coffee table between us
all my bottles lined up.
He asks, How are you feeling? –
and then he picks up the bottles
and looks at them.
Are you all right for those?
You want some of these?
He writes out two prescriptions.
I'll see you in three weeks' time.

There is no examination.
You have to be dying
to get an examination.

Pills

I'd love to throw them all away –
I have two damn bagsful –
but when I stop the pain comes back:
shoulders, knees, ankles, the lot.
I was taking twenty-three tablets a day –
surely that's not for the human body –
heart pills, liver pills,
god-knows-what pills –
and I don't even have heart trouble!

Keeping Going

I was never unemployed except for five days
I volunteered to join the army
but I was chased out – unfit for service –
RAOC, rejected army of Christ

I was so fit –
played rugby, horse-vaulting,
weight-lifting, wrestling,
you name it –
but I had brucellosis
I was collecting milk
seven days a week for two pounds ten shillings a week

They sent me home from hospital
the lieutenant loaned me ten shillings
I never repaid him
they were sent to Tripoli
I would have gone too
I never saw them again

But I would have rather been dead
because I was so ill
I had to hold both hands over my stomach
in case anyone touched it

After that my wife died
left me with a daughter seven months old
now she doesn't want to know me –
that's one of the hardest things –
when I wrote to my daughter
she wrote back:
'We have had no contact for a number of years,
I feel we should leave things as they are.'

It's a wonder we keep going
but we do, don't we, you and I
we bounce back.

Pain

It's the pain keeps me awake
I never know which leg it's going to be –
it comes down my thigh to my knee
then to the top of both feet
then into my toes.

I've got arthritis of the spine
no sight, cancer of the colon
half-paralysis of the face
inflammation of the arteries:
is there anything else left?

Ivy Poxon

The Czech poet Milosz said writing poetry was like trying to harness a tiger. I think Ivy is fighting a lot of tigers. She sits in Smokers' Corner puffing away, elbows and knees at the ready. You never know, if you're Ivy, what blow will come next. Abused, deserted, broken, I fear, in body and spirit; as a barmaid she has seen and heard more than her share. 'I could write a book,' she says, 'but it would be censored.' I am not here to console or whitewash; I just write down what she says. Impassioned utterances; bitterness; sadness. I wish she would write that book – I'd help her – but I know she won't. The tigers have sapped too much of her strength.

She is oddly pleased to see her words transcribed (I thought she might be angry: she thinks I'm sneaky the way I take down what she says). But 'That's how it was, that's how it was,' she says. I think she's relieved to find those awful feelings can be borne, that they don't burn holes in the paper. She asks if she can have copies to keep in her handbag.

They were there when she died.

Roaring Tide

I'll tell you something I used to do –
watch the tide coming in at Morecambe
waves beating up against the sea wall
water coming up at me –
it was when I had a pain,
when somebody had hurt me
I'd wait for the tide coming in
to wash it away
I'd stand there
until all the pain had gone.

My temper was coming out of the sea.

I went and stood on the Prom
thinking, to be honest, about suicide.
Especially if the sea was rough
I loved it
knowing it wasn't hurting me
or anybody.

Heartbreak

She wasn't a mother to me.
I don't know what a mother is.
I'm fifty years old.
The only thing she's ever done for me was when I was born.
I never told her that I'd been poorly
She wouldn't have been interested.
This time I said, I need you.
She said, You could have killed me the way you're talking –
And I'm the one gasping for breath.

I didn't believe anybody could be like that.
She's all for herself.
It's the first time I asked her for something.

I was always wrong, right from the beginning.
I shouldn't have been there.
I'm still paying for it, aren't I?
Instead of one heartbreak
she's given me two.

Morning

I

I was watching two rabbits at six thirty
and hanging over the toilet at seven thirty.

II

It's the best time of year
you can sit and watch
and enjoy the peace
nobody's there disturbing it
then you get a bloody car
comes along and frightens it.

Terry McCormick

These poems are here
Because
I sent them
To Lynne
My friend
&
Co-conspirator
She said
I would
If you would
I said
You could
She's the editor
I wrote them
She chose them
I ordered them
&
Wondered . . .

During her residency
I was fixed in grief
&
Now
These poems are here

The First Place

Snow sweeps Pen Pica –
Here was conceived
The Family of Dreams.

This is the point –
All children play.

Rowan – his childhood
Slammed away
Is in our arms
Blood whitening to ice.

The kissing gate
Opens a path
To the summit.

The Last Days

Rowan's body breaks down.
Not beautifully as in Autumn
Dawns following a cycle of rain,
But terribly
When you consider the beauty
Born out of the first days.

Yes, this soul may be leaving
But not slip sliding away
Gently; no.
Physical wreckage
Is thrown everywhere.

Where is the emergency cord?
How can I snap
The catch on the ejector seat
So we can float into darkness
Together on a bed of space –
Souls travelling
Without the body of pain?

When I consider my dying son
As part of the psyche we share
And try to figure, make sense;
All thoughts arrest.

He is a dream of salvation
From the guilt of a decided death;
He is a dream of justification
For the love and hate of a lifetime;
He is an adventure to pitch
The drag of history
Into the flattest of spins.

When I consider my son's death
As the death of the child born
From me I argue
For the miracle
Which lives through all our stories
And that my son's story
Is now for the telling
Outside his sojourn
In the body of our lives.

Then against these words
I rage tears and tears
For would I not love
The embrace with a body
Wracked to shivers deathly
Than the clasp of a soul
Pure, wingless, and flying free?

Wishing Gate

Before the Wishing Gate
A mottled woodcock
Revs out of John's Grove.

Under Loughrigg
A green caterpillar
Swings across the path.

I remember the Black Rabbit
Skipping away
On the coffin track.

And then how my heart's
Heart aches always
Through Deerbolts Wood.

Gladys McCartan

'That one will talk to you,' says Sister Callistus, indicating a lumpish old woman with a mean-looking snarl and a droopy right eye. Not the kind to meet in a dark alley.

No one escapes the Gladys-mangle: men, women, daughters, dogs, doctors; me; herself. The eye may droop but rarely the tongue. Sometimes I'm a little afraid of her. Perversely – because she is so verbally gifted – she will not allow me to exhibit her poems. 'Private,' she hisses, curling her lip. 'Besides, it isn't any good. Nobody will want to read it.' Her daughters convince her otherwise. Humph, she says, but relents.

She sings a Welsh song for me; tells me how only Welsh words can express certain meanings: longing is a yearning from the heart. I bring her a copy of Bruce Chatwin's *On the Black Hill* but she's too ill to read it.

I tell her she reminds me of my mother. 'Is that right?' she says. The one eye. 'She too was a fighter, a philosopher; she didn't give a damn about possessions.' She nods at my baggy culottes (approval at last!). We try on each other's floppy crocheted hats. She looks beautiful in hers; she tells me I look like Paddington Bear in mine, 'Thanks a lot,' I say.

Has Gladys been sent to test me? I shouldn't spend so much time with her, it isn't fair. Maybe I'm making up for not being with my mother at the end.

I thought my mother would live for ever too. Gladys is brave enough and trusts me enough to tell me she's afraid. 'You're fond of all of them but some you get more attached to than others,' says Sister Maureen.

Mother: Christmas, 1971

She was crippled, bedbound, isolated,
nothing to do but face the window.
She said to the doctor, 'I'm ready to go anytime.'
'What do you mean?'
'Close your eyes and that's it.'
'Oh no, dying isn't that easy,
it's hard work,
you don't die when you want.'
She lived for a week:
she didn't drink, she didn't speak,
she was as dry as a whistle.
She got hold of my hand
gave it an occasional squeeze
to say: I know you're there.

It was on a Friday morning.
I had to go to the shop
I left the back door open for the doctor
I was away only five minutes.
When I got in it was too late:
she'd gone.
It was Christmas, 1971.

Mirror

I looked in the mirror
And I saw what I saw
When I fall asleep I'm young
In my memories I'm young.

Jiggered

I'm jiggered – you know what that means?
My Dad used to sit with one leg
over the arm of a chair.
I'd say, 'How are you today, Dad?'
and he'd say, 'I'm bloody tired – jiggered.'
We never realised that he really was.

It's more than tired
I'm jiggered.

His Master's Voice

I

When we were kids
we used to go to a place
called Maes-y-hafn –
the field of the haven.
It was a house in the country
where all the chickens
used to jump on windowsills.
Ooh, here comes flapperwings, we'd say.

We sang or played the spoons,
Auntie Maggie brought down the gramophone –
His Master's Voice.
We'd have 'Hallelujah Chorus'
and 'Son of the Mountains':
 'Away from home I'm making a song
 My heart is in the heather
 With all the small birds and rippling brook.'
Those were the kind of records we'd listen to

II

Christmas Day, kids' day
nurses on the ward
we were bored
said, let's have some fun
let's put a piece of slabcake
on the record
until it suddenly came off
and we would laugh
and laugh
and laugh

III

My friend Agnes cleaned out the shed
it was a lovely warm summer's day
they brought the antique dealers
but nobody wanted the gramophone.
We sat on this old bench up the back garden
laughing our heads off.
All those old records:
'Yes, We Have No Bananas'.

If You Can't Turn It Upside-Down and Sit on It, Throw It Away

A man came to the door:
have you anything to sell?
I had a rocker –
nobody's behind was sitting in it;
there was a chest –
it was going out of fashion:
so I sold them. How was I to know
he'd sell them for twice as much?

Now I could live in a cell:
you know what brought me to that?
Living here. It was that woman Rene,
always having her hair done,
her nails painted, made red.
She had a lot of money,
a fancy house. But I thought:
what the heck did she need all that for?
She can't look after that anymore.
She had to sell. She had to give up
what she treasured, all her furniture.
I can't hoard things, not me.
People buy something to make them richer
but it's of no value when you're ill.

Illness brings you down quite a peg or two.

When you're young you like nice things;
when you're old you don't want to be bothered.
If it's not good, throw it away;
if you can't turn it upside-down
and sit on it – throw it away.
That's what I say.

Arthur Marshall

Arthur is ninety years old. He was never ill until five years ago when everything started to go wrong at once. He thinks it has to do with losing his wife after all those years together. She was the one who did the talking; he relied on her. But he has quite a lot to say for himself. He talks about the transience of things; how they don't make woollens the way they used to. As for him, he hurts, he's worn out, he's tired. He smiles, 'I'm ready to go now.'

Made to Last

I have a suit at home
it's charcoal colour
I got it for my mother's funeral
it's like new
I only wear it for funerals.

I have an Abercrombie overcoat
it was bought in 1938
right thick
you don't feel any wind
it will never wear out –
not like people
not like me.

Scalded

When I was two and a half I was scalded –
I'm going back to 1903 –
right from my leg right round.
I went into fits,
the shock made me stammer;
it took me thirty years to recover.
It did something to me,
took my self-confidence off me:
when I used to go in company
I used to watch people's faces,
if they wanted me:
I've always gone in the background.

Big Boy

I've always been a tall lad for my age
I never got a ride on a rocking horse
At work they gave me jobs beyond my years
I thought it were marvellous
What a big boy am I.

Keith King

Keith sits in his wheelchair describing something called 'lamping': he and neighbouring farmers go out in their cars in the middle of the night with powerful spotlights plugged into their cigarette lighters; in the quiet they sit and watch foxes, owls, deer, badger, everything. His face lights up as he remembers. He has a heartbreakingly sweet smile which he turns on (rather like lamping?); it fades as soon as he's alone. 'I used to run up and down those fields in my shepherd boots but I can't do owt now,' he says. Keith has worked on farms up in the Lakes since he was a lad. Five years ago his dream came true: the 300-acre farm near Grasmere where he worked came on the market. He and his wife bought it but before the paperwork was completed he was diagnosed as having multiple sclerosis. They went ahead anyway.

Keith is powerfully built and deeply tanned from working outdoors on the farm (he supervises the work on a motorised tractor). When he's at the Hospice, where he comes when his family go on holiday, he sits brooding, smoking, only just managing to contain his frustration.

Keith thinks I'm 'right bossy'. He keeps trying to slip clichés into his writing. I don't think he'll ever forgive me for editing out 'jewels in the sun'. He is as pig-headed as they come. When I tell him his poems are good he says, 'I don't call them poems I call them stories.'

New-cut Grass

I was riding along on my bike –
a three-wheeler farm bike
only smaller with big bubbly tyres –
a special disabled bike.
I was down at the stream
I switched the engine off
I stopped for a smoke and a think.
All I could hear was the sound of the leaves.
The stream was running low
and you know how they make a rippling sound,
the sun was on the minnows
they were darting about
to me with no purpose:
they must have a good purpose for doing it.
As I looked up there were two hares
sparring like boxers do.
I could see the shadow of a bird
hovering in a warm thermal.
As I turned to go home
there was an old Reynard
looking for a cool safe place –
he'd know where he was going
he'd know if there was an old empty drain,
even hounds couldn't get to him up there.
Before I got home I could smell **new-cut grass**.

Dumb Dog

Sometimes I sit
Sometimes I just sit and think
Sometimes when they say
What have you done today?
I wish I could get up and walk away.
People stand behind you
You're twisting your head around
They won't look you in the eye
People will pat you like a dog
I'm not a dumb dog.

Heavy Snow

The quietest time I ever knew
was when it started to snow half-crowners
We were walking out in it
to fetch some sheep off high ground
You couldn't hear a thing for the snow
All you could hear was the cracking
of the tree branches
It was frightening really
going up through the woods –
they were cracking like guns.

Lamia and Ibtissam Kholoud

Sisters – one little, chubby and dimpled, the other tall, thin and solemn. Both beautiful. Their mother is in the Hospice with a brain tumour. Their grandparents bring them to visit several times a week. It's one of those warm, early summer evenings. I'm sitting in the Hospice courtyard peacefully reading my book when the two delicious honey-coloured dolls in matching striped sundresses and fuzzy pig-tails turn up. 'Can we play out here?' Go ahead, distract me. They take turns pushing each other round and round the flower beds on a blue plastic lorry. When she's had enough of that Lamia climbs up on one of the sun chairs and forces her bottom through the plastic slats. Ibti, watching, remarks, 'I do believe she's going to teach people to fall through holes.' Now there's an interesting profession!

Ibti means to write about the statue. She circles round it, working from surface detail to interior meaning, from cobwebs to comfort. Her approach to writing, as it is to life, is exact and thorough. 'Maybe you'll be a writer when you grow up,' I say. 'Could be.'

Giggles as they forget, knitted brows as they remember; silly songs and poems followed by frowns and stricken consciences – so it goes round and round like the blue plastic lorry. 'Faster faster faster,' yells Lamia.

I Was Afraid

Behind my Mum's Hospice is a large house that nobody lives in. Lamia and I had a bit of trouble walking up the field to get there. When we got to the top we saw a large messy garden and a grey house and we saw that there were wooden planks covering the doors. But there was one plank that was loose so we looked inside. There was a noise inside but it was only a bird. I walked on but Lamia kept making silly noises with sticks and buckets. We both felt afraid. Lamia kept finding secret passages. Then a black bin bag started to move. We thought it was a witch! So we ran back to the Hospice. Grandad put *Neighbours* on. Me and Lamia felt safe in the day room and away from the big house.

The End.

Ibtissam

Dear Mummy,

I wish you have a happy day
I wish you get better soon
I wish you get lots of flowers
   daffodils
   pansies
   red tulips
I wish you get home soon
   to our house in Levens
   to the big garden with swings in it
I wish you could sit in the garden
   and listen to me play my fiddle
I wish you get lots of visitors
   ones who sit for a long time
   ones who'd be with you
   and talk to you
   and listen to you
   the way I listen to you.
I wish you have a happy life.

Love,

Ibtissam

My Sister

My big sister is really really bossy
and she's mostly writing and reading.
She sometimes listens to her Walkman
and she's sort of slim.
She's really really big
and she's heavy
and she makes bets
'I bet you plants don't grow in a week'
and she likes coming to see Mummy.

Lamia

My Mummy

My Mummy used to not be in hospital
but now she is.
I like her
she's wonderful
and Grandma and Grandad go to see her
every day.
We go when we've got time
and mostly we go to school.

Lamia

Sad Statue

It's quite tall
It's got two people on it
The people have no shoes on
They're kneeling and sitting down
They're holding close together
They've got holes for their eyes
but they don't have any eyes
They're wearing long robes
There are cobwebs all over them
and tiny red ants
They're not very colourful
They look quite solemn
An accident might have happened
They look as if they're kneeling at an altar
They look as if they're comforting one another
after the accident
I think she feels sad because of the accident
but she's started to smile
because she is being comforted.

I would like to be comforted like that
because I lost a penny that was very old
I would like to be comforted after Lamia
knocked me with the badminton racquet
I would like to be comforted
because Mummy is ill
and because she is not with me.

Ibtissam

The Statue

They look nice and holy
and they've got holes for their eyes
It's all made of stone
and they've got long robes on
Their colour is not bright
because it's a dark black
They're standing on a kind of table
and they've got bare feet
They look like they're sad
and it's a man and a woman
They seem to be holding each other
and I think they're husband and wife

Lamia

Paul Harvey

We live from holiday to holiday and then, boom, it's just about staying alive. Paul was about to go off on an expedition to K2 when he found the lump in his neck. The doctors said he couldn't go.

But he has managed to stay alive and more. He is fit and getting fitter all the time. He got married in the spring. But as he says, he's come out of his illness rather like a badger coming out of the dark.

Paul is almost disturbingly honest about his illness. He doesn't try to prettify. He isn't afraid to look me or anyone in the eye and say, this is how it was.

Now he'd like to write about other things besides illness – life, love, nature, politics, his own patients (he's a psychiatric social worker) – but it doesn't come easy. There is an ambivalence, a strand that wants to celebrate life and then that other one, that old blinking badger, that needs to revisit the dark.

Treatment Day

I awake from the sleeping tablet:
Is it Wednesday again?
Treatment day and I feel sick already.
I sit in the bath clutching a book on
rock-climbing and try to read.
I say to myself:
'all I ever have is this moment now'
and so I try to relax in the moment.

Stephanie drives me to hospital.
I have a bowl ready for the journey home.
In the waiting room I breathe deeply to keep calm.
'We've got the drugs from pharmacy,
we're ready for you now, Paul.'
I slip on to the treatment couch trying not to
notice the drip.
Which hand will it be this time?
The gentle sister's gloved hands rub my veins
and a little prick and I am snared again.
A wave of sweat pours off my bald head.
I want to jerk out the tube and run –
run anywhere but here.
My arm becomes frozen as the cold liquid
snakes its way into my body.

My veins will later feel burnt.
I can taste the drugs in my mouth now
and retching clutches at my throat.
I am being poisoned to save my life.

A few hours later I am being driven back home.
I am terrified of all the traffic,
of our car being smashed into,
for it seems to me that anything is possible now.

Back at home the curtains are drawn.
I curl up in bed with a hot-water bottle.
Everything feels so black I cannot even bear music.
The children will be quiet about the house
for the next few days, for in a few hours –
I can even set my clock by it – the vomiting
will begin and I can start pissing
away the cancer.
I look forward to my sleeping tablet.

Three Faces

I did not know any of your names.

A man in his thirties perhaps.
You had a surgical collar about your neck
and a small plastic box on your chest, flashing a red light
for pain control I think.
You were sitting in the hospital bed colouring in a picture.
It seemed to me a strange thing to be doing here.
You told me things were rough
and all I was able to say was 'Take it easy.'

The second was a woman with dark eyes
and black curly hair.
I was lying on the treatment couch
wired to the drip, wishing I was anywhere but here.
It was all taking oh so long
and you, you couldn't stop talking.
You were in pain and frightened, I know
but you just couldn't stop talking.
You said that you felt safe here in the hospital
as if nothing could happen to you.

I was with other cancer patients in a group at the Hospice.
There in the corner was a young lad
in his blue dressing gown.
You looked like I did ten years ago –
thin, shy, nervous with glasses. Bewildered. Overwhelmed.
I couldn't understand what you were doing here with us.
I thought it was some silly mistake.
I wanted to go over and say something to you
but I did not know what to say.

The three of you died in three weeks.
You are all dead, and I am alive.
And I don't know why.

The Treatment Couch

There is a problem.
Relatives have donated money for a treatment couch.
A plaque must be placed recording the memory.
But how to do so without upsetting us?

Out of sight underneath
on one of the cross-arms
the name is placed.

We patients can still see it though.
We are not stupid and I don't think we mind.
We are not upset by it.
The mind is concentrated a little further.

Judith Hall

Hospice means a resting place for the sick and for travellers seeking refreshment for the spirit. For me as a nurse it's also a place of rest and renewal. Dying is a chance to put things right – a time to say 'I'm sorry' or 'I love you' or 'I'm afraid'. The Hospice is a place where it's OK to say these things, to talk about dying. This gives me strength; it helps me face my own mother's death.

Judith Hall

Four Fragments

He liked to be first in the bath.
'Don't you want to finish your tea?'
   'No thanks, it's cold, stewed and strong!'
The bath was run
His bubbles were gone.
'Oh dear, it's not your day, Keith.
Your tea's cold, stewed and strong
and your bubbles have gone.'

Another time –
   The one who was so particular
   about her appearance;
   she was only 82 –
was asked,
'Would you like some soup?'
'What kind is it?'
'Lentil.'
'Mental – oh no thanks
I'm mental enough' (and she chuckled).

It was only a week ago
he sketched my face.
Now the talent has gone and only
the picture remains.

I remember Gladys who said one morning,
'We all ought to be shot.'
    'Shall I bring it round this side?'
    I asked, indicating the tray.
'What,' she said, 'the gun?'
(and we laughed together).

The Other Side of the Doors

It was me dressed in grey silk culottes
and black wool sweater – off duty.
I took a wheelchair patient
back to the ward, his bedmate
was amazed to see me dressed like that.
Could I turn on the power for the TV?
Suddenly everyone was wanting
something.
For twenty minutes no one had been
around.
Suddenly everybody looked at me –
me dressed as somebody else –
   not in white;
   but a person;
Next bay I looked
There were three sleeping patients
   the third was lying awake –
turned – lying – wanting
complaining – that vulnerable state –
I walked past.

David Gorst

Did the doctor take his own medicine? Well, yes – but he nearly had to be held down! Writing is difficult enough even when the subject matter is under firm control – a scientific paper, for example – but when the tussle is with the feelings and emotions which surround illness and dying it is very easy to become much too busy for that sort of thing.

The doctor wonders why he does what he does – what drives him. Is it pity? a defence? a ritual magic to prevent any of those dreadful things happening to him? Has he found the perfect way to combine salving his unease at contemplating illness with avoiding even the idea that *he* may get sick, may need help? (Doctors' bizarre attitude to their own illness is well known.)

We doctors are not used to having to expose ourselves in the same way as patients and the exposure involved in this sort of writing is considerable. It was dreadfully difficult and I don't think much of the results. Was I showing solidarity with the patients? Keeping Lynne happy? I am not sure. I learned a lot and I think the message is that it is okay to drop your guard: nothing dreadful happens and some good may even come of it.

℞

Take my knowledge, accept my understanding
Take my needles, lost in the greater hurt
Take my advice, consider my opinion
Take my tablets, my red and blue infusions
Heave and vomit but come back for more
Take my sympathy, my support, my despair
Don't ever ask me how I am

I Touch the Mountains Lightly

I touch the mountains lightly
The warm valley exhales, easing me up to the cool stones
The shapes change but I know them
Their mass comforts me

This Doctor's Dilemma

It is more blessed to give than to receive . . .
It's also a whole lot easier
Filling needs is a wonderful excuse
For not doing other things
Difficult disturbing things
Like yielding, like accepting
Like confronting feelings.

I have no grace
I am tough
I don't need help from anyone.

John Fletcher

John the cynic never wrote anything in his life besides love letters to his wife and reports for his job. This isn't poetry, he insists; poetry is Wordsworth. Yet he keeps dictating; and denying; dictating and asking me to read back what he's written; and denying. One day I catch him in a mellowish mood. 'Well, do you think they're poems now?' I ask. He shakes his head but keeps smiling. Would I mind reading them just once more? He leans back in his wheelchair. 'I still don't think it's poetry,' he says.

Pat III

I remember Mollendo
I remember the office
I remember the *nombrada*
of the stevedores outside the office
I remember walking home one night with Pat
when three men appeared on the other side of the road
I remember taking Pat's hand and saying
'When I say run, you run'
I remember one of the men left the others and walked
    towards us.
He was a big man.
I recognised him as one of the stevedores
I remember him saying, '*Ola Gringo*!'
I remember there was no more worry.

The Perfect Circle

The most beautiful thing I ever saw
was a bridge over a stream –
half-circular.
The reflection of the bridge
was so symmetrical.

There was nothing on the track.
We were quite alone.
Would that I could see the bridge again.

Pat II

I remember walking Pat home
through the dark streets of St Helens.
She was not afraid and I felt stronger.
No one would touch her with me.
Past the park and down the hill
hand in hand along Sandy Lane
to her home, number 28.
She was never afraid
not of me or anyone
and I'm so pleased that she wasn't.
We would stand by her gate
then she would go till the next time.
I loved her
I still do.

Gordon Elliott

Gordon comes to the Hospice twice a week. As befits the former deputy head of a local junior school, he sits at the head of a long table or plays billiards. I figure he doesn't need my help: he can write poetry without me. I'm wrong, of course; he hasn't written anything for a long time. He needs someone who will say more than, 'That's nice, Gordon.' We do not always agree. He thinks I disapprove of rhyme (I don't: I just think you have to be a minor genius to use it well). I encourage him to be freer and more direct about his feelings. Take this, for example:

> Listen to me
> when the Inner Rage seeks to express itself.

I ask him what he's trying to say. 'Why me? Why should it be me that's suffering?' 'Good, that's much better. Why not put that down?' So he does. Now we're getting somewhere.

The Stone

One lonely afternoon I walked by a stream.
My foot kicked a stone. I picked it up.
It was long and almost round.
I washed the grey stone in the clear
running water. It turned black.
As I caressed the contours and
indentations of the stone
I realised it resembled a nubile female form.

Later I glued the stone to an oval flat base,
then I varnished it.
The black shining statuette now stands
on the top of my writing-desk cabinet;
a figure of interest for various reasons
to our circle of friends.
But no one knows what it meant to me.

Listen to Me

Listen to me.
Why should this have happened?
Why should it be me?
Why should I be suffering?
Why me?

Listen to me when I speak
Of the yearnings of my
Heart.

Be kind to me.
Understand me when I cry.
Believe in me when
I speak my thoughts.

But what can I say
That will be worth remembering?
Perhaps a few well-chosen words,
Perhaps nothing.
It would all depend
On the listener.
It would – if only
The particular person
Allowed my words
To stir the imagination.
But how many times does this happen?

Kath Dinsdale

What's a flour grader? Add details and colours, the names of places – it helps to bring the poem alive. 'Glass pendants and earrings, floppy hats, floral headscarves' . . . good, good. My instructions, my enthusiasm. Kath manages a small, pained smile, apologises for her sleepiness which she explains is due to an injection for pain control. At first her eyes remain half closed; she hasn't the energy to open them. She wears a grey dress; her skin is also dun. I don't know if this is going to be possible.

She tells me her son writes poetry, that she admires it but cannot do it herself. What would she write about? I say, picture someone special to you; begin each line 'I remember'; you don't have to think too hard about it, just make some word images.

She finishes the poem, then opens her eyes fully and smiles before dozing off again.

Grandma

I remember sailing across the River Mersey to visit Grandma
I remember Grandma waving to me when the boat came to dock.
She was big and round and cuddly
she used to crush me
I used to get lost in her breasts
she used to call me her lovely girl.

I remember shopping with Grandma
and afterwards she'd buy me a large cream bun.
She used to knit for my doll Sambo
little suits she used to knit
little shoes.

I remember going with Grandma to the swings in the park
and writing to tell my mother and father all we'd done
I remember trying on Grandma's jewellery
glass pendants and earrings
floppy hats
floral headscarves
I remember sneaking Grandma's powder puff
till I looked like a flour grader
I remember telling Grandma secrets –
she used to listen
she was good at listening.

I remember Grandma because I loved her very much
and how she loved me too.
I can remember doing the washing with Grandma
putting the soap on collars and cuffs
weeding the garden
walking along the beach at New Brighton
collecting shells.

I remember sailing across the River Mersey
to tell them all about Grandma.

Grandma's Cat

I remember Grandma's cat
he was called Sooty
he was black
he used to sleep on the piano
   on the keyboard
   so I couldn't play it
he fell asleep on my half-made jigsaws
he would spit at me when I tried to move him
he could be very friendly when I was eating
he'd rub round my legs purring
   trying to scrounge a little of my meal for himself.

I used to try to smuggle him up to my bedroom
   so he'd be there as company during the night
I could only manage if the terms
   were right for him.

It's funny that they should have cared about one another, Sooty and Grandma.

She would have given everything to make you happy. He would have taken the lot.

Dorothy Cullen

'I'm a Lancaster girl,' she says proudly. Dorothy worked as manageress of Famous Army Stores for fourteen years. She was shy and unconfident; she lived an isolated life. She and her husband Fred have no children. Two years ago Dorothy was told she had cancer.

Her life changed. There was no crashing of cymbals, no going off to a Zen monastery, no rainbows or revelations. It was just – I say just – a quiet shift in which her world, as she says, opened up.

Dorothy comes to St John's every Monday. She sits with her legs up amongst a group of women who do craftwork. She is at home, accepted. She almost always has a smile on her face. When she first came to the Hospice she wouldn't say a word. 'Now they can't stop me.'

Why Do They Say It?

I was in the Infirmary,
one of my neighbours saw me.
She said, 'Oh my god, not you Dorothy.'
I was admitted on Tuesday,
operated on Wednesday.
I had no say in the matter.
The worst part was going home and telling Fred.

I thought I was the only one:
you feel so alone,
a dreadful feeling inside,
you can't go on with life
there's nothing there.

Later I went to Christie's.
I made friends at Christie's,
we had some happy days.
We used to go out for a meal
or down into Manchester City Centre:
it was a very happy time at Christie's.

I'll never be afraid again
but at the time I was terrified.
I didn't know anything,
what to expect.
If they tell you more it helps you realise,
it helps you face it better.

The worst part is when you come out.
Some speak to you, some don't.
They say, 'Oh look,
there's that poor girl's got cancer.'

Why do they say it?

You Can't Be the Same Again

When I first went to the Hospice
I wouldn't say a word –
now they can't stop me.
I have so many friends –
my world has opened up.

I'd never be able to get Fred out –
now we go every Thursday:
we look around the shops together
we note the price of things.
He's so content.
We get pleasure out of doing it together.

We laugh and joke more;
I don't snap, I'm more tolerant.
Last week Fred dropped a cup of tea.
Before I'd have created,
now we can laugh:
there's something every day.

It does make a difference –
the shock of hospital,
the mastectomy.
It hits you so much:
you can't be the same again.

Janet Corkill

Janet answers the telephone at Reception. She is the first, and sometimes the last, person I see each day at the Hospice. Even though we don't know one another very well, Janet is an accurate barometer of my moods. 'Ooh, she's a thundercloud today, watch out.' 'It's a good one today, she's bright and bouncy.' She gets a kick out of trying out Americanisms on me. At the end of the project she presents me with a splendid gadget that will stamp 'Have a nice day!' on my morning toast (I shall think of her with every bite!).

'People think it's only nurses are interested in patients. It's not true. The domestic girls and us, we care what happens to someone. We get something out of it too. Everyone who works here gets more than they give.' Janet turns the common assumptions upside-down. Why should patients be grateful for the care they get? 'I think it's big of people to let themselves be helped. We're the ones who get a big kick; the patients are only getting the love and attention they deserve. The really good person is the sick one who allows the Good Samaritan to help them.'

Telephone Callers

Wish I could see you, you on the telephone
Wish you were here
All my telephone calls keep coming
Wish I could see you
Wish you were here (like the TV programme)

Trouble is I can't see your face
I can't tell if you're getting angry
When I can't find the right person
The one you really want to speak to
I can't tell if you're putting on a brave face
When you ring up all crisp and efficient
To make enquiries about your mother
Are you bleeding inside?

When you ring I want to know what you look like
Are you a little bloke who wishes he was taller?
Are you in a wheelchair and you really hate it?
Are you a great big cosy lady with a great big bosom
Reaching out to cuddle the world
To give the world a big cuddle?

Trouble is, if I could see you
You might not make the call at all
You might get all self-conscious and not say half you do
You might hold back on me

Anne Charlesworth

'"The whale", quotes Anne, "has the biggest brain ever created and a fifty-million-year-old smile." And you think, where are you? Are you worth that much? The answer is, No I'm not.'

Anne is thirty, blonde, beautiful, smart, talented. She's had one breast removed and now the cancer has spread to her spine. Meanwhile she's engaged in a philosophical and spiritual quest. 'Disease is a guru,' she says, 'an opening of the doors, the way in.' She claims it's the easy way to learn; she has a sense of being pushed by her illness. 'Towards what?' I ask. 'Enlightenment,' she replies, beaming like a svelte Buddha.

When I Die

Put me in a black plastic bag
And secure it with an elastic band above my head.
Why destroy a noble tree
(More worthy in the world than me)
Because you think that I am dead.

Drip

Ward 3 Annexe
Lying on the couch
Constant hum of the drip monitor
Drip inserted into left hand
Drip drip – so slow
Don't watch the drip bag
Seems like nothing's happening
There is only here
There is only now
Only the drip bag going down.

On Finding a Lump in my Neck

Beauties just discovered
Months of contemplation
Sudden revelations
Truths found. And then –
In one split second
Fingers exploring my neck
Everything falls apart.

A lump no bigger than a pea
But longer than the earth itself
No stars, no heavens, no universe
Just me – and my lump.

The Polar Bear at Chester Zoo

I am locked in my body,
You are locked in your pit.
I lie and dream of melting into clouds.
As you pace – forwards, backwards,
Your head lolled, rolling side to side
Your tongue hanging between your teeth –
Are you dreaming
Of cold blue skies and polar ice caps?
We watch you – your body in its sick disturbing rhythm
But are you really there?

[The polar bear has since been destroyed.
I hope it has found its freedom.]

Julia Bukowski-Burrill

Jules the nurse. She comes to my office carrying an envelope bursting with song lyrics. I sit and listen while she tells stories about old ladies behind lace curtains, spooky houses, flowers and whales and dogs and birds and . . . Her eyes glitter as she leans forward, quoting and singing. She is bursting with creativity and health; impossible not to make the obvious comparison.

More and more thick wadges shoved under my door.

Jules is one of those multi-talented people – art, music, writing – the form hardly matters. All I do is listen, suggest sharpening the focus on her poetic camera – click, it's all there. 'If you hadn't walked in, it might never have come out,' she says. Not true: it was there already. But we can all do with a little encouragement.

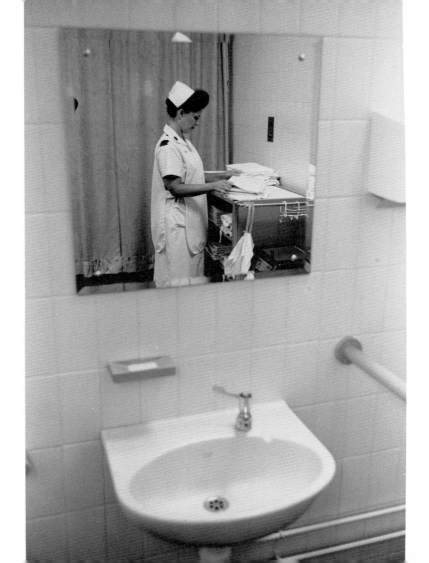

Journey

He looked ready
  for dancing.
He wore
  a bright silver
  striped
  waistcoat
  bow-tie
  smart trousers.
The shine on those shoes!

He looked ready
    for dancing
    lying there
    in his coffin.

Tucking Away

She was sewing buttons
on to a nightie
with such precision
the act
was almost sensual
as she deliberated over stitches
with swollen fingers . . .

After so long to do
something
with her time.

She ploughed her whole being
into those openings
tucking away discreetly
in material.

As I Passed Her Room

Almost as if
taking in the sun
   she sat there
decompression sleeves
   wrapped around her legs
   like floats.
Yes, she could have been
   floating
      somewhere . . .
   iced water waiting
   beside the pool.
Almost as if
   taking the sun
   she sat there
   eyes closed
      behind glasses
   the summer heat
      penetrating the windows
      in her room.
Perhaps she was
   sailing for a time
   down untroubled waters.

Lynne Alexander

Why Should I Be Included In This Book?

I don't have cancer
I'm not a doctor
I'm not a nurse
I'm not a receptionist
or Sister of Our Lady of the Apostles
I'm no poet

On the other hand,
my mother
my father
my brother
are dead
and my ex
might as well be

and anyway
these popped out.

The White Hat

[for Gladys McCartan]

Sitting on a beach at Hersonisos
Dress hiked up, striped umbrella cocked,
Feet planted in sand, ready for anything:
Gladys in white hat with rose

Now it sits on her bed
collapsed and roseless
Who cares, it's lovely, I say
Oh come on, she says,
pushing truth to the last
OK, Gladys, it wouldn't do in a punt
No, it didn't even keep the sun off in Crete.

The Colour Yellow

[for Bishop Cross]

What shall I call him: Your Grace,
Your Reverence, Your Lordship?
Please, call me Stewart. Okay.
Stewart, I like your daffodil pyjamas.
Yes, they match my eyes.

He shows me an arm:
Inadequate, he says,
blood too thick.
This weakness is like a black hole.

Hooked up to lines, transfused,
What am I?
Christ was at his strongest
nailed to a cross.
And what am I?

He closes his eyes, shamed,
says he's not a volatile man.
I don't mean to be presumptuous.

Writer in Residence: The Passing of a Year

Summer, USA. I teach students to write
Water plants, feed cats, sunbathe.
With my notebook on my knee
I sing, *Oh don't you cry for me.*

Autumn, UK. Write letters
To my computer. He's handsome,
Charismatic, well versed in literature.
Unfortunately he doesn't reply.

Christmas. Hang a bunch of mistletoe
With high hopes and red string.
Wait for somebody to be tempted:
The mistletoe waits too.

Spring, Great Langdale. Still waiting.
Will he come over the mountain?
The cuckoo thinks not
Couples in hiking boots: ditto.

Summer, the Hospice. Travel down-Ward
Holding pen, holding hands:
I'm afraid to be alone; afraid to take a nap . . .
Fears into verse: we call it making art.